清乾隆京城全图局部

Detail of the Sketch Map of Beijing, the Imperial Capital (the Reign of Emperor Qianlong, Qing Dynasty)

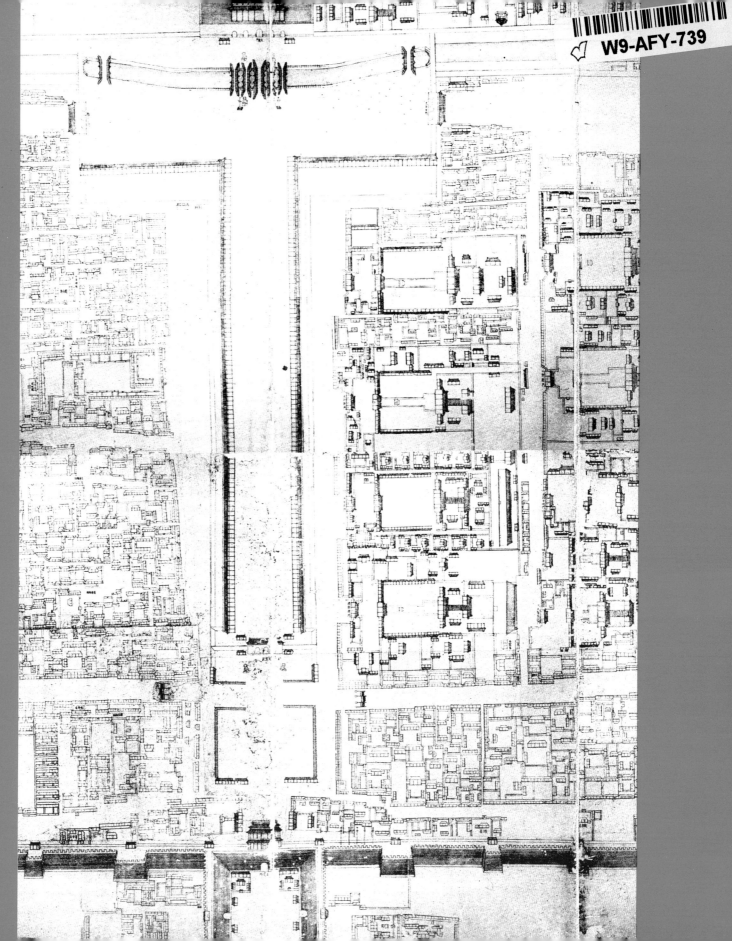

顾　　问:	侯仁之	Consultants:	Hou Renzhi
	赵　洛		Zhao Luo
封面题字:	沈　鹏	Front Cover Inscription:	Shen Peng
题　　词:	吴良镛	Inscription:	Wu Liangyong
主　　编:	翁　立	Chief Editor:	Weng Li
编　　委:	翁　立	Members of the Editorial Board:	Weng Li
	丁幼华		Ding Youhua
	张承志		Zhang Chengzhi
	张肇基		Zhang Zhaoji
责任编辑:	张肇基	Editor-in-charge:	Zhang Zhaoji
装帧设计:	张承志	Designer:	Zhang Chengzhi
撰　　文:	翁　立	Written by	Weng Li
英文翻译:	麦仰曾	Translator:	Mai Yangzeng
摄　　影:	丁幼华	Photographers:	Ding Youhua
	张承志		Zhang Chengzhi
	许延增		Xu Yanzeng
责任印制:	赵　恒	In Charge of Printing Affairs:	Zhao Heng

北京的胡同 沈鹏篆

北京美术摄影出版社·北京· Beijing Arts and Photography Publishing House

图书在版编目（CIP）数据

北京的胡同＝HUTONGS OF BEIJING ：画册：
中、英文对照/翁立主编—北京：北京美术摄
影出版社，1993.4
ISBN 7—80501—160—5

Ⅰ．北…

Ⅱ．翁…

Ⅲ．①胡同—北京—摄影集 ②建筑史—北京—图集

Ⅳ．TU—881.21

北京美术摄影出版社出版
北京市北三环中路6号
邮政编码：100011
电话：010-62013123
010-62028146
北京出版社总发行
精美彩色印刷有限公司制版印刷
1997年10月第1版第5次印刷
印数：22501-28000
开本：787×1092毫米 1/12 印张：8
ISBN7-80501-160-3/J·156
006000

吴良镛先生题词
Inscription by Mr Wu Liangyong

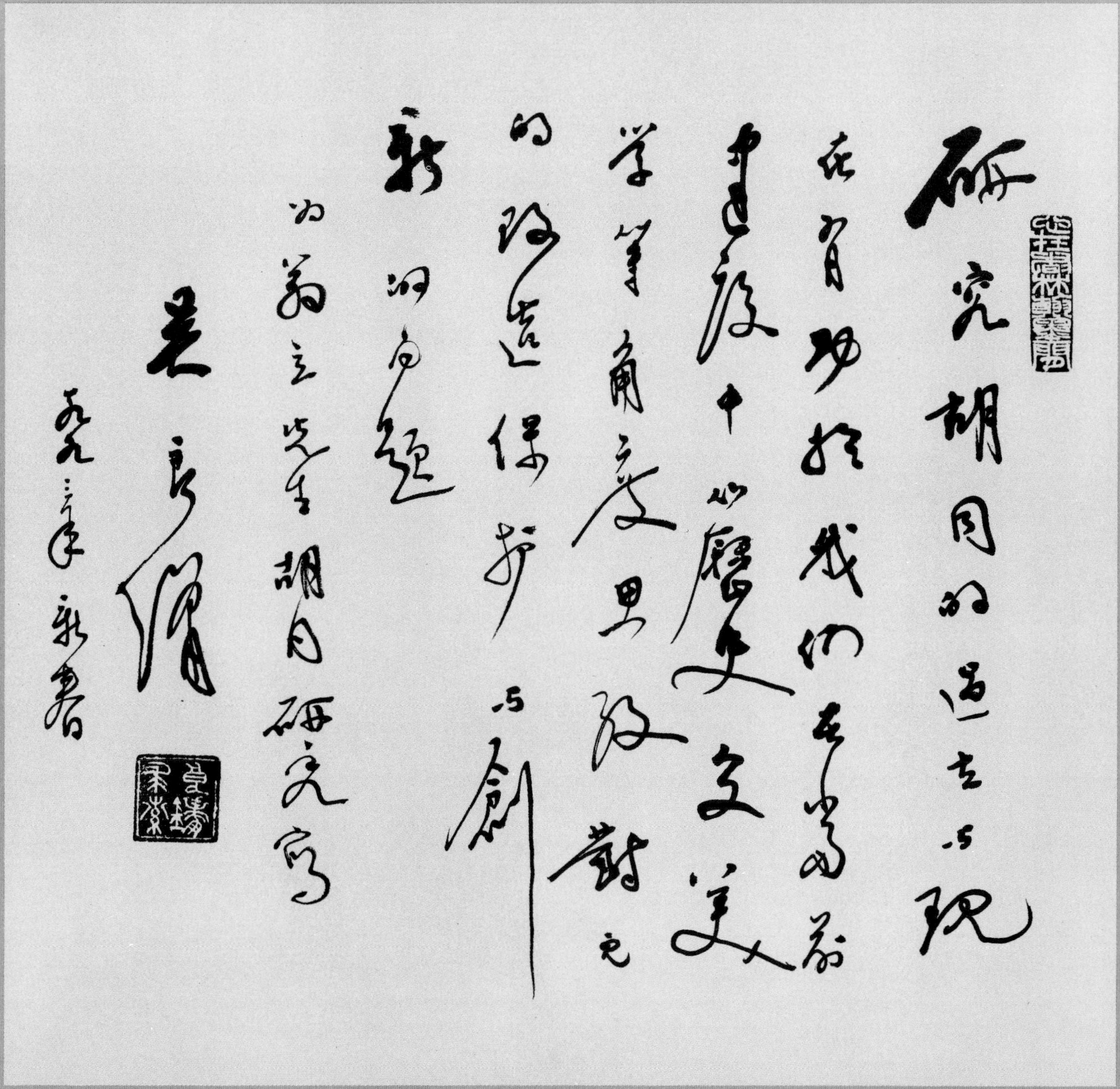

研究胡同的过去与现在有助于我们在当前建设中以历史、人文、美学等角度思考对它的改造保护与创新的问题。

为翁立先生胡同研究写

吴良镛

一九九三年新春

Studies on the past and current situations of Hutongs will help much in considering the questions of the protection and creation about them from the angles of history, humane and aesthetics when engaging in construction projects nowadays.

Written for Mr. Weng Li's Research on Hutongs

Wu Liangyong

Spring of 1993

目　录
List of Paintings

锁链胡同
Suolian Hutong

新街口七条
Xinjiekou Qitiao

前　言

　　北京，不仅是中国的历史文化名城，也是世界文明史上最壮丽的文化奇观之一。不用说那举世闻名的天安门、金碧辉煌的故宫、雄伟壮观的长城，就是那一条条看上去很不起眼的小胡同，里边的学问也大着哪!

　　乍一看，北京的胡同都是灰墙灰瓦，一个模样。其实不然，只要你肯下点功夫，串上几条胡同，再和那儿的老住户聊上一阵子，就会发现，每条胡同都有个说头儿，都有自己的故事，都有着传奇般的经历，里面的趣闻掌故多着哪。

　　因为北京的胡同绝不仅仅是城市的脉络、交通的衢道，它更是北京普通老百姓生活的场所，京城历史文化发展演化的重要舞台。它记下了历史的变迁，时代的风貌，并蕴含着浓郁的文化气息，好象一座座民俗风情的博物馆，烙下了人们各种社会生活的印记。漫步其中，到处都是名胜古迹，细细品味又似北京的百科全书，不少胡同中的一块砖、一片瓦都有好几百年的历史了。从史籍中看，光是"胡同"一词的写法从元朝到清朝就有：衖通、火弄、火疃、火巷、火衖、胡洞、衖衕、衕衕、俉衕、忽洞、湖洞等十多种。

　　北京胡同的形成是随着北京城的形成而变化、发展、演进的。大约在五十万年前，这块地界儿开始有了原始人居住，不过那时只是住在天然洞穴而已。到了距今大约一万到四、五千年间，这儿出现了原始氏族公社，开始住上了简易房屋。到了三千多年前的公元前1045年，这儿成了奴隶制的古燕国的都城，叫蓟城，可当时的城墙只是用夯土筑成的。到了战国时期，广为流传的《周礼•考工记》明确规定："匠人营国，方九里，旁三门，国中九经九纬，经涂九轨，左祖右社，面朝后市。"可见那时已非常注重城建制度了，就连城中街道布局都作了明文规定。以后的两千多年间，从秦、汉开始，无论是三国、两晋、南北朝，还是隋、唐、五代和宋朝，这块地界儿一直都是北方的重镇。十世纪初，辽朝建立，把这儿当成了陪都，改称南京，又称燕京。公元十二世纪，金朝建立，在此建都，称为中都，中都城里出现了坊、街、道、巷，但至此还没有"胡同"出现。

　　公元1276年，元朝在毁于战火的金中都原址东北部，按《周礼》之原则建立了"状如棋盘"的大都城。并于1285年2月"诏旧城居民之迁京城者，以赀高及居职者为先，乃定制以地八亩为一分；其或地过八亩及力不能作室者，皆不得冒据，听民作室"。贵族功臣，悉受封地，以为第宅。于是，元朝的官僚、贵族们就按此规定，在大都城内盖起了住房及院落。这一间间房屋、一个个院落，一个挨一个盖起来，连起后就是一排排的，而一排与另一排之间要采光、通风，还得留出进出的通道，便形成了胡同、小街和大街。据元末《析津志》载："大都街制：自南以至于北，谓

宫门口横街
Gong Men Kou Hengjie

5

东四牌楼旧照
An Old Photograph of Dong Si Pailou

之经;自东至西,谓之纬。大街二十四步阔,小街十二步阔。三百八十四火巷,二十九衙通。衙通二字本方言。"当时的大都城是元世祖忽必烈的天下,这方言当然就是蒙语了,本系"水井"之义。有水井的地方才有人烟,才得以居住。且当时盛行的杂剧戏词中,也不止一次提到"胡同",如关汉卿的《关大王独赴单刀会》中就有"直杀一个血胡同";再如李好古的《沙门岛张生煮海》中说得更具体:"你去兀那羊角市头砖塔胡同总铺门前来寻我。"可见北京的胡同是形成在元大都城的格局里。不过元大都当时仅记有29条胡同,因当时明确规定宽9.24米的才叫胡同,要是达到18米宽就叫小街,到36米宽就称为大街

了。

公元1403年明朝的燕王朱棣当了皇上,将这儿改称为北京,这时才有了"北京"这个名称,至今已叫了590年,但比"胡同"这个名称晚出现了一百多年。并开始大规模营建北京城,城墙一改以往用土夯筑的方法,而是全部用砖包砌。大城里包着皇城,皇城里包着紫禁城(今故宫)。紫禁城位于京城中心,而紫禁城的中心又是皇极殿(今太和殿),皇上的蟠龙宝座又位于皇极殿的正中。有一条无形的线从这个宝座上穿过,它就是北起钟鼓楼南至前门楼,后又延伸到永定门,纵贯京城南北,长达16里的中轴线。整个北京城的建筑布局,都是以此为依据的,城内一切

建筑都整齐对称地排列在其左右,街道胡同也如此,或对称排列在它两边,或与之平行。这种布局充分体现了尊帝王、崇皇权、重礼仪、右文化、敬天地、法祖宗的思想。公元1420年北京城营建完工,明成祖正式迁都北京。公元1553年,又增建了城南外垣,至此北京城又有了内外城之分,北京城的"凸"字型平面布局至此基本定型,面积约为62平方公里。内城九门,外城七门。这时北京城的胡同,据《京师五城坊巷胡同集》载:有街巷711条,胡同459条,共为1170条。

清朝定都北京后,完全沿用了明北京城,就是后来也只是对紫禁城和皇城进行了一下小的改建、重修。但由于清是女真族的后裔满洲贵族

金鱼胡同旧照
An Old Photograph of Jin Yu Hutong

金鱼胡同
Jin Yu Hutong

建立的王朝，所以定都北京后便实行了空前绝后的旗、民分城居住制度，令内城居住的汉人全部迁到外城，这样就促进了原来较为冷清的外城的发展。新迁至外城的人又匆匆盖了许许多多的新房、新院，连起来就形成不少大大小小、长长短短、规范或不规范的新胡同。此时对原来元朝作的胡同必须宽9.24米的规定，早已逐渐模糊了，虽街巷胡同格局"大抵袭元、明之旧"，但"街巷"与"胡同"的界定早分不那么清楚了，总体数目已增到2077条之多。

辛亥革命结束了清朝的封建统治。民国前期北京仍是中华民国的首都，1928年国民党南京政府把北京改为北平特别市。过去由于皇城占了北京城的中心位置，因而阻断了东西主干线，东西往来必须绕道天安门广场以南的棋盘街或北边的地安门。民国初年，随着紫禁城的开放，行人才可以横穿东西长安街。这样，北京就有了一条和纵贯南北的中轴线直角相交横穿东西的长纬线。经纬相交于天安门前，形成一个大十字坐标，街巷胡同就以此为中心而往外发展开。几条新干道的打通、增辟，带动了胡同的发展，到四十年代北京的街巷胡同已达3200多条。

但胡同面貌真正改观，还是解放以后。1949年改北平为北京，为中华人民共和国的首都。从此，北京这座历史文化名城发生了翻天覆地的变化，城市建设日新月异。到八十年代中期，北京全市总面积是过去老北京城的24倍，其中市

北京胡同中遗存的英文水泥路牌："RUE HART"(赫德路)，是90多年前帝国主义侵占东交民巷地区的罪证，它时刻提醒人们不忘国耻。

The cement street nameplate with the name "RUE HART" is the evidence of the fact that imperialists forcibly occupied the Dong Jiao Min Xiang Area over 90 years ago. The plate always reminds people of the national humiliation.

达智胡同
Da Zhi Hutong

西四北三条中的程砚秋故居
Former Residence of Cheng Yanqiu in
Xi Si Bei San Tiao

北半截胡同中的谭嗣同故居
Former Residence of Tan Sitong in Bei
Ban Jie Hutong

魏染胡同中的京报馆，是著名报人邵
飘萍主办《京报》的地方
Jing Bao Guan in Wei Ran Hutong,
Which Was the Site Where Shao
Piaoping, the Famous Journalist, Set
Up the Newspaper《Jing Bao》

米市胡同中的康有为故居
Former Residence of Kang Youwei in
Mi Shi Hutong

区建成区比解放初扩大三倍多。新建各类房屋面积，相当于建了五个旧北京城。这么一来，胡同数目比解放前增长了一倍，已有街巷胡同6104条，直接称为胡同的仍有1316条，且环境也变得整洁幽美，更重要的是胡同的内涵随着旧城墙逐步地拆除，也变得更广泛了。北京不仅新建起许许多多的高楼大厦、居民住宅生活小区，同时也在进行着改造旧街、小胡同的建设。许多胡同名称虽依然如故，但大都早已不是旧日模样了，一些胡同中的危旧平房早被单元小楼所替代了。比较典型的如东城菊儿胡同、西城小后仓地区出现的四合院式住宅楼，不仅使居民的住房条件有了根本改善，而且保持了十足的"京"味儿。为保护古都风貌，维护传统特色，北京城区还划定了二十余条胡同为历史文化保护区，像南锣鼓巷、西四北一条至八条等就被定为四合院平房保护区。自元大都以来形成的老北京胡同的棋盘式格局正在与二环、三环、四环等环形加放射布局联系在一起。胡同的面貌既古老又年轻，古都风貌与现代风姿在这里相映成趣，相得益彰。

胡同的形成和发展，在其名称上也留下了历史变迁的痕迹，并反映出社会风情。每条胡同一形成，人们自然会给它起个名，这个名称一旦被大多数人所接受，叫开了，就确确实实地代表了这条胡同在整个城市中的方位，成为人们交往、通信等活动中不可缺少的标志。这是胡同名称的实用指代作用。由于胡同名称从元朝开始形成胡同起，一直都只是靠人们口头相传，至于用文字写在标牌上挂在胡同口上，只是民国后才有的。因而好多胡同都是以一个较明显的形象标志来命名的，这也表现出北京人的实在、直爽和风趣，象较宽的胡同，人们顺嘴就叫成了"宽街"、窄的就叫"夹道"、斜的就叫"斜街"、曲折的叫"八道湾"、长方形的称"盒子"、短的有"一尺大街"、低洼的有"下洼子"、细长的叫"竹竿"、扁长的称"扁担"、一头细一头宽的为"小喇叭"等等。早年间，最显眼、最突出的标志就要数城门、庙宇、牌楼、栅栏、水井、河流、桥梁了，所以就出现了以此命名的西直门内、外大街、前、后圆恩寺胡同、东四(牌楼)、西单(牌楼)、大栅栏(老北京人读成：大市腊)、水井胡同、三里河、银锭桥胡同等胡同名称。有的小胡同附近没有这些特别显眼的标志，胡同中种的树多，就有了柳树胡同，枣林胡同，椿树胡同等以树命名的胡同。许多胡同在起名时为了好找，还在胡同名称前加上了东、西、南、北、前、后、中等方位词，象东坛根胡同、西红门胡同、南月牙儿胡同、北半壁胡同、前百户胡同、后泥洼胡同、中帽胡同等。

因为胡同名称是住在胡同里的北京人自发起的，所以有不少北京的土语在里边，象背阴儿胡同、取灯儿胡同、闷葫芦罐儿胡同、筲帚胡同、胰子胡同、嘎嘎胡同等。还有不少胡同带有儿音，更显得京味儿十足，象罗儿胡同、鸦儿胡同、雨儿胡同、土儿胡同、帽儿胡同、盆儿胡同、井儿胡同等。

有些胡同名称还能表露出人们的美好愿望，人们总乐意用一些吉利的字儿来给胡同起名。象带有什么"喜"啊、"福"啊、"寿"啊等字眼的胡同就有喜庆胡同、喜鹊胡同、福顺胡同、福盛胡同、寿长胡同、寿逾百胡同等等。还有带着"平"啊、"安"啊、"吉"啊、"祥"啊字眼的平安胡同、安福胡同、吉市口胡同、永祥胡同等等。还有富于浪漫色彩的胡同名称，如百花深处、杏花天等，也有可笑的狗尾巴（老北京人读作"狗乙巴"）、羊尾巴（羊乙巴）胡同等等。

而象文丞相胡同、张自忠路、赵登禹路等胡同的名称都是人们为了纪念民族英雄而命名的，从而明显表达了人们对民族英雄的敬慕。这就说明胡同的名称绝不仅仅只有实用的指代作用，还具有美学功能和人文倾向。

有的胡同名称从元朝一直叫到今天也没有什么变化，像砖塔胡同就是一例。从明朝叫到如今没有什么太大变化的还有门楼胡同、罗儿胡同、翠花胡同、绒线胡同、头发胡同、松树胡同、史家胡同、灯草胡同等三十多条。可许多胡同的名称却随着改朝换代，而一再变更着，最多的一条胡同竟会有五、六个曾用名。象现在宣武门外的菜市口胡同，明朝时本叫绳匠胡同，清朝乾隆年间讹传为神仙胡同了，后又讹传为丞相胡同。也有些胡同名称，本来取得比较粗俗，后来一点点逐渐改文雅了，如驴市胡同改成了礼士胡同、猴尾巴胡同改成了侯位胡同、鸡爪胡同改成了吉兆胡同、瘦肉胡同改成了寿刘胡同、屎壳郎胡同改成了时刻亮胡同、臭皮胡同改成了寿比胡同、牛血胡同改成了留学胡同等等。这些基本上都是以意思好的同音字，取代了不好听的字。属谐音转换，而且叫起来与原音又差不多，胡同里的人们都乐意接受，因而就能流传开来。但如果未经广大群众认可，强加给人们的，就不会叫响，如文化大革命时在极左思潮影响下，把一些带有明显标语口号式的字眼强安在胡同名称上，象把戴家胡同改名为红哨兵胡同、将北豆芽胡同改名为红小兵胡同、将豆角胡同改名为红到底胡同、把珠市口西大街改名为红卫东路等等，结果只叫了一时，很快就消逝了。这就说明胡同名称也并不是谁随随便便就能给改了的。

可也有些胡同名称，其历史沿革的关系意义实际上已经失去，如琉璃厂已不再烧琉璃瓦而变成书业文物集中的文化街、煤市街也已不卖煤、菜市口已不卖菜、米市胡同已找不到米市了、鹁鸽市也已不见鹁鸽了，但其旧名称却一直到如今还在这么叫着。究其原因，就是因为与人们日常生活还是密切相关的。

后圆恩寺胡同中的茅盾故居
Former Residence of Mao Dun in Hou Yuan En Si Hutong

护国寺街中的梅兰芳故居
Former Residence of Mei Lanfang in Hu Guo Si Jie

珠朝街中的中山会馆，是孙中山先生1912年来京时到过的地方。
Guild of Zhongshan County in Zhu Chao Jie
Where Dr. Sun Yat-sen Visited in 1912 When He Came to Beijing

北京的胡同名称看上去包罗万象,既有江河湖海(大江胡同、河泊厂胡同、团结湖、海滨胡同)、山川日月(图样山胡同、川店胡同、日升胡同、月光胡同)、人物姓氏(张自忠路、贾家胡同)、市场商品(菜市口胡同、银碗胡同)、工厂作坊(打磨厂、油漆作胡同)、花草鱼虫(花枝胡同、草园胡同、金鱼胡同、养蜂夹道)、云雨星空(云居胡同、雨儿胡同、大星胡同、空厂)、鸡鸭鱼肉(鸡爪胡同、鸭子店、鲜鱼口、肉市街)等等,名目繁多,令人看着眼花缭乱,但如果认真分析,还是有其自个儿内在的规律的。

北京的胡同名称,实际上是以人为中心的,有的胡同直接以人名来命名。也有不少胡同虽没以人名来命名,但其中却有名人故居,像米市胡同里有康有为故居、北半截胡同中有谭嗣同故居、珠朝街有孙中山先生到过的中山会馆、小杨家胡同是老舍先生的出生地、护国寺街有梅兰芳故居、后圆恩寺胡同有茅盾故居、西四北三条有程砚秋故居等等。而其它各类胡同名称虽不是直接以人名来命名的,但也都与人们的日常生活有着直接关系。人们的生活离不开衣、食、住、行、乐,所以更多的胡同就以此来命名了。北京胡同名称大体上可以分为四大类:(一)以人名命名的胡同;(二)以市场商品命名的胡同;(三)以建筑物命名的胡同;(四)以地形景物等来命名的胡同。

这本画册就采撷了近150幅照片,从不同角度来反映这四大类胡同的风貌。因篇幅所限,各类只能选编进一小部分。我们只想通过这些,使广大读者朋友能对北京的胡同有个概略了解。

东交民巷的天主教堂
Catholic Cathedral in Dong Jiao Min Xiang

东四三条夜色
Night View of Dongsi Santiao

东吉祥胡同
Dong Ji Xiang Hutong

FOREWORD

Beijing, one of the famous historic and cultural cities of China, is also one of the most magnificent cultural miracles in the history of the world's civilization. Not to speak of the world-famous Tian'anmen, the resplendent and magnificent Former Imperial Palace and the imposing Great Wall, even those unattractive Hutongs (lanes) arouse much reveries and it takes a lot of learning to explore into their developments.

At first glance, all Hutongs in Beijing are formed by lining buildings with gray walls and gray tiles. But in fact, it is not so simple. Spend some time wandering through some of them and chat with those old inhabitants, then you will find that every and each Hutong has something to be talked about. They all have their respective stories which tell about their legendary vicissitudes from which you can learn much interesting episodes and anecdotes.

Hutongs of Beijing are decidedly not only the veins of the city and the thoroughfares for traffics, but also the site where common people live, and the important arena of the historic and cultural developments and evolutions of the Capital. Marking the historical vicissitudes and features of different stages, and containing rich cultural flavour, they are like museums of folk customs and popular charms, and preserve the stamped brands fo people's social life. When wandering in the city, you will find scenic spots and historic sites almost scattering everywhere among Hutongs and think,

after careful savouring, that they are like an encyclopaedia about Beijing. In many Hutongs, you can find pieces of bricks and tiles which are several hundred years old. According to historical records, the name "Hutong" had been written, between Yuan and Qing Dynasties, in more than a dozen of forms (such as "Hongtong", "Huolong", "Huotuan", "Huoxiang", "Huohong", "Hudong", etc.)

Hutong of Beijing had formed, changed, developed and evolved after the changes of the form of the city. About 500000 years ago, primitive men began to reside in a natural grottoe on the site. About 10000–4000/5000 years ago, primitive clan commune appeared and people began to live in simply constructed houses. In 1045 B. C. (which was over 3000 years ago), the site became the capital of ancient Yan (a state under the slave-owning system), and was called the City of Ji. It was a city with city walls built with rammed earth. By the Warring States Period, as distinctly recorded by the widely spread 《 Rites of Zhou·Technical Standards》 (Zhou Li: Kao Gong Ji): "Craftsmen constructed the Capital with surrouding wall 9 li in circumference, and 3 gates were open on the wall. The city was divided by 9 longitudinal lines and 9 latitudinal lines, and the longitudinal roads were 72 chi wide. Imperial Household Shrine was on the left and Shrine of the God of Earth on the right. In front was the imperial court and marketing place was behind". Such records indicate that much attentions were paid to the system of urban constructions, and even the layout of the streets in the city were also clearly set. In the ensuing over 2000 years, including the reigns of Qin, Han, Three Kingdoms, Western and Eastern Jin, Southern and Northern Dynasties, Sui, Tang, Five Dynasties and Song, the place had always been a place of strategic importance in the north. In the first years of the 10th century A. D, the newly founded Liao Dynasty set the place as its secondary capital and renamed it Nanjing, or Yanjing. In the 12th century, Jin Dynasty made the place its capital and renamed it Zhongdu. In those days, the streets in the city were called by such names as Fang, Jie, Dao and Xiang, rather than Hutong.

In 1276, Yuan Dynasty had a large capital which was laid out "like a chessboard "built, according to the principles set by 《 Zhou Li 》, on a site northeast to Zhongdu which had been destroyed by wars. An imperial edict was promulgated on February, 1285, saying that" Among old inhabitants of the city who wish to move into the Capital, those who are rich or in high positions will be given priority. 8 mu of land are taken as the standard. Those possessing more than the standard amount of land, or those being unable to build houses, are not allowed to take the chance. Then, common people can build their houses and reside there. Nobles, and officials who made meritorious contributions, are all granted land to construct their residences." Thus, bureaucrats and nobles of Yuan Dynasty built residences with courtyards in Dadu according to the regulation. Neighboring houses made up lines and rows of residences. For the purposes of daylighting and ventilating, as well as to leaf out passages for entrances and exits, Hutongs, streets and roads were gradually formed. As recorded in 《 Xi Jin Zhi 》 which was published in the last years of the reign of Yuan, "The layout system of Dadu consists in Jing (south-north oriented) and Wei (east-west oriented). Large streets are 24 bu in width, and small ones 12 bu. There are 384 Huo Xiang and 29 Hong Tong. The term Hong Tong is from dialect." Then, Dadu was under the jurisdiction of Kublai Khan, Emperor Shizu of Yuan Dynasty, the dialect undoubtedly referred to Mongolian. Hong Tong meant "water

well". People could live only where there wells were dug. The term Hutong appeared repeatedly in verses of then prevailing operas. A line in the aria of 《 Guan Yu Going to the Banquet with His Broad Sword 》 reads "Going to fight through a bloody Hutong." Names became more exact in a line of 《 At Shamen Island Zhang Yu Set Fire to the Sea 》 (an opera written by Li Haogu), which reads "Find me at the shop in Zhuan Ta Hutong, Yang Jiao Market". These show that Hutongs of Beijing were formed in the setup of the City of Dadu of Yuan Dynasty. However, there were just 29 Hutongs in Dadu because it was clearly regulated that Hutongs were passages with a width under 9.24 metres, while those with a width up to 18 metres were called Xiao Jie and those up to 36 metres Dajie.

In 1403, Zhu Di, Prince Yan of Ming Dynasty, became emperor. He had the name of Dadu changed into Beijing. Beginning to appear 589 years ago, the name Beijing came out over--100-year later than the appearance of the term Hutong. Then, large-scale construction projects began in the city of Beijing. The city walls built by rammed earth were all surfaced by large bricks. The outer large city surrouded the imperial city which surrounded the Purple Forbidden City (Present-day Former Imperial City). Purple Forbidden City was located at the centre of the capital, Huangji Hall (present-day Taihe Hall) stood at the centre of Purple Forbidden City and the imperial throne was set at the centre of Huangji Hall. An invisible line, the 16-li-long axle, starting from Bell and Drum Towers in the north and reaching Qianmen Tower in the south (stretching to Yongdingmen later on), passed over the throne. The axle line had been the base of constructional layout of the whole Beijing city. All constructions in the city were set neatly and symmetrically on either sides of the line. Street and Hutongs lined on either sides symmetrically or in parallel orientation. Such a layout symbolized the conception of attaching great importance to emperors, imperial authorities, rites, culture and of following the undertakings of ancestors. The construction project of Beijing was completed in 1420, and Emperor Chengzu of Ming Dynasty formally

moved the capital to Beijing. A ring of outer wall was then built to the south of the city, thus Beijing was divided into the inner and outer cities, and the "凸" formed city of Beijing was fundamentally fixed. The area of the city was about 62km². There were 9 gates on the inner city walls, and 7 on outer ones. According to 《 A Collection of Fangs, Xiangs and Hutongs in the 5 Districts of the Capital 》, there were 1170 passages (including 711 Jies and Xiangs, and 459 Hutongs) at that time.

After setting its capital in Beijing, the Qing authority had kept the city of Beijing intact, just making small-scale re-buildings or renovations at times on the Purple Forbidden City and the imperial city. But as Qing was a dynasty established by Manchurian aristocrats who were the offsprings of the Nüzhen nationality, an unprecedented and unrepeatable system of separative residing between the Han nationality and bannermen had been strictly undertaken. People of the Han nationality, who formerly resided in the inner city were all moved to the outer city, prompting the development of the comparatively desolated outer city. Rows and lines of new houses with courtyards were built by people who moved to the outer city, so that new Hutongs of different sizes and lengths, standardized or not, appeared. The regulation from Yuan Dynasty that the width of Hutongs was limited to 9.24 metres had become vague gradually. Though "the setup from Yuan and Ming Dynasties had generally been kept", the distinction between Jie/Xiang and Hutong had already become blurred. The number of the passages totaled 2077.

The Revolution of 1911 concluded the feudal ruling of Qing Dynasty. In the first years of the Republic of China, Beijing was the capital of the newly founded country. In 1928. KMT Government in Nanjng had Beijing turned into Special Municipal of Beiping. In the past, the east-west major traffic line had been blocked up by the imperial city locating at the central area. People had to go by a roundabout route through Qipan Jie to the south of Tian'anmen Square, or passing Di'anmen in the north, when they wanted to go from the east city to the west, or vice versa. People could go passing east and west Chang'an Boulevard only after Purple Forbidden City was open to the public in the beginning stage of the Republic of China. Then, a long latitudinal traffic line which linked up the eastern and western parts of Beijing and perpendicularly intersected the vertical central axle came into existence. The point of intersection locating at the front of Tian'anmen formed a large cross coordinate which became the centre of out-spreading passages. Several new trunk lines were open up or newly built, speeding up the development of Hutongs. By the 1940s, the number of passages in Beijing amounted to over 3200.

However, actual changes of the appearance of Hutongs occurred only after Liberation. In 1949, the name Beiping was changed to Beijing, the city has become the Capital of the People's Republic of China, earth-shaking changes have taken place in the famous historic cultural city ever since, and the appearances of urbanic constructions changed day by day. By the middle stage of the 1980s, the total area of the city has come to 24 times over that of old Beijing. The completed urban area amounts to over 4 times as compared to that at the beginning stage of Liberation. The area of newly built houses equals to that of 5 old Beijing. Thus, the number of Hutongs has been doubled. The number of passages now amounts to 6104, among which 1316 are called by the term Hutong, and the environments have become clean, tidy and graceful. What is more important is that the connotations of Hutongs have become wider as the old city walls are gradually removed. Innumerous high buildings and residential areas have been completed, while reformations of old streets and small Hutongs are under way at the same time. Though preserving old names, many Hutongs present new appearances. Dangerous one-storeyed houses in many Hutongs have long been changed to apartment houses. Typical cases include Ju'er Hutong in east city, storeyed residential buildings in the form of a quadrangle, and many other. In all these places, not only residential conditions are fundamentally improved, the traditional flavour of Beijing are also well-preserved. In order to protect the attractions of the ancient capital and to preserve traditional features, over 20 Hutongs in urban district are

宫门口三条
Gong Men Kou Santiao

appointed historic and cultural protection areas, such as Nan Luo Gu Xiang, Lanes NO.1 to No.8 to the north of Xisi, and others, which are listed as Protection Areas of Quadrangle One-storeyed Houses. The chessboard setup of Hutongs in Beijing formed since Yuan Dynasty is now combining with the circling and projecting layouts on the Erhuan, Sanhuan and Sihuan Roads. The circling and projecting layouts are old and new at the same time, and the appearances of the ancient capital are set off by modern styles.

The formation and development of Hutongs show traces of historical vicissitudes on their name, and they reflect social inclinations. When a Hutong is formed, people will assuredly give it a name. When the name is accepted by the majority, and prevails among the public, it exactly represents the location of the Hutong in the city, and becomes the necessary symbol for people's intercourses, communication and other exchanging activities. Such is the practical indicative function of the names of Hutongs. After Hutongs were formed in Yuan Dynasty, their names were just passed on orally by people. Beginning from the Republic of China, they were printed on boards which were hung separately on ends of related Hutongs. Thus, many Hutongs

were named separately by distinct imaginal symbols. This also shows the dependability, straightforwardness and wits of the people of Beijing. To take some examples: A broader Hutong is called "Kuan Jie" (Broad Street) offhandedly; for a narrow one, "Jia Dao" (Narrow Lane); for an oblique one, "Xie Jie"; Ba Dao Wan for a zigzagging one; "He Zi" (Box) for a rectangular one; "Yi Chi Da Jie" (A One-chi-long Street) for a short one; "Xia Wa Zi" for a low-lying one; "Zhu Gan" (Bamboo Pole) for a long and thin one; "Bian Dan" (Carrying Pole) for a flat and long one; "Xiao La Ba" (Little Brass-wind Instrument) for one broader at one end and thinner at the other; and so on. In the past, the most outstanding symbols were those for city gates, temples, monuments, railings, wells, rivers and bridges. Hence the names of Xizhimennei Dajie, Xizhimenwai Dajie, Qian Yuan En Si Hutong, Hou Yuan En Si Hutong, Dongsi (Pailou), Xi Dan (Pailou), Da Zha Lan (read as Da Shi Lar by old residents of Beijing), Shui Jing Hutong, San Li He, Yin Ding Qiao Hutong, and so forth. For small Hutongs without outstanding symbols around but possessing a certain number of trees, names like Liu Shu Hutong, Zao Lin Hutong and Chun Shu Hutong were given. To provide strangers with

东四十条中的垂花门 (垂花门原是四合院内的二门，东四十条扩建后，才露于街面)
A Chui Hua Men (Decorated Gate) in Dong Si Shi Tiao (The gate was originally the inner gate of a quadrangle. It became the main entrance of a house after the lane was enlarged)

菊儿胡同中四合院式居民楼
Residential Building in Quadrangle Style (Ju Er Hutong)

东四三条的早市
Morning Market in Dong Si San Tiao

富强胡同
Fu Qiang Hutong

义达里
Yi Da Li

高筱胡同
Gao Xiao Hutong

convenience in finding their. required Hutongs, positional terms were frequently added to the names, such as Dong Tan Gen Hutong, Xi Hong Men Hutong, Nan Yue Yar Hutong, Bei Ban Bi Hutong, Qian Bai Hu Hutong, Hou Ni Wa Hutong, Zhong Mao Hutong, etc.

As the names of Hutongs are mostly given by native people of Beijing who live there, a considerable amount of colloquial expressions are taken separately in them, such as Bei Yinr Hutong, Qu Dengr Hutong, Men Hu Lu Guanr Hutong, Tiao Zhou Hutong, Yi Zi Hutong, Ga Ga Hutong, etc. Many other present rich flavour of Beijing by the suffixation of a nonsyllabic r in them, such as Luor Hutong, Yar Hutong, Yur Hutong, Tur Hutong, Maor Hutong, Penr Hutong, Jingr Hutong, and so on.

Some names present fine aspirations by auspicious wordings of "Xi" (Happy), "Fu" (Fortune) and "Shou" (Longevity), such as Xi Qing Hutong, Xi Que Hutong, Fu Shun Hutong, Fu Sheng Hutong, Shou Chang Hutong, Shou Yu Bai Hutong, etc. Ping An Hutong, An Fu Hutong, Ji Shi Kou Hutong, Yong Xiang Hutong and many similar ones are also included. Names like Bai Hua Shen Chu and Xing Hua Tian sound romantic, while Gou Wei Ba (read as Gou Yi Ba by native people of Beijing) Hutong and Yang Wei Ba (Yang Yi Ba) Hutong are funny.

Names like Wen Cheng Xiang Hutong, Zhang Zizhong Lu and Zhao Dengyu Lu are given to commemorate national heroes, presenting people's admirations for them. As such, names of Hutongs are decidedly not only given practical indicative function. They also possess aesthetic function and humane inclination.

Some names have been kept intact since they were given in Yuan Dynasty, among which Zhuan Ta Hutong is exemplary. Over 30 names have existed since Ming Dynasty without much changing, including Men Lou Hutong, Luor Hutong, Cui Hua Hutong, Rong Xian Hutong, Tou Fa Hutong, Song Shu Hutong, Shi Jia Hutong, Deng Cao Hutong and others. However, many names changed repeatedly following dynastic changes, and at the most, 5 or 6 names had been given to a Hutong at different times. For example, present-day Cai Shi Kou Hutong outside Xuan Wu Men was called Sheng Jiang Hutong in Ming Dynasty, but was spread erroneously into Shen Xian Hutong during the reign of Qianlong in Qing Dynasty, and again changed erroneously into Cheng Xiang Hutong later on. Some Hutongs had originally a vulgar name and changed gradually into refined ones. For examples: Lü Shi Hutong was changed gradually into Li Shi Hutong, Hou Wei Ba Hutong into Hou Wei Hutong, Ji Zhua Hutong into Ji Zhao Hutong, Shou Rou Hutong into Shou Liu Hutong, Shi Ke Lang Hutong into Shi Ke Liang Hutong, Chou Pi Hutong into Shou Bi Hutong, Niu Xue Hutong into Liu Xue Hutong, and so on, Such a way of change Was widely adopted in vicissitudes of Hutongs. These are fundamentally all homonymic changes—homonymous characters with auspicious meanings take the places of ones with vulgar meanings. These changed words are easily acknowledged and accepted by inhabitants in the related Hutongs, and can be spread smoothly all over the city. Forced names without being acknowledged by the people can not exist long. During the "Great Cultural Revolution" and under the influence of the ultra-"Left" trend of thoughts, some term with evident slogan styles were forcibly put into names of Hutongs, such as: Dai Jia

雪后神路街
Shen Lu Jie after Snow

Hutong was changed into Hong Shao Bing Hutong, Bei Dou Ya Hutong into Hong Xiao Bing Hutong, Dou Jiao Hutong into Hong Dao Di Hutong, Zhu Shi Kou Xi Dajie into Hong Wei Dong Lu, and so forth. They prevailed for only a short while and vanished very soon. It showed that even the names of Hutongs could not be changed at random by Zhang, Li or anybody.

For some names of Hutongs, their relative significance of historical evolutions has actually lost. For instances: Liu Li Chang is no more the site where glazed tiles are fired, but a cultural street where the trades of books and cultural relics concentrate; coal is not sold at Mei Shi Jie and vegetables not in Cai Shi Kou; rice market is not to be found in Mi Shi Hutong and doves are not seen in Bo Ge Shi. But the names still prevail. It is because that they are closely linked to people's daily life.

Names of Hutongs in Beijing seem to be all-embracing—They involve river, lake and sea (Da Jiang Hutong, He Bo Chang Hutong, Tuan Jie Lake, Hai Bin Hutong); mountain, the sun and the moon (Tu Yang Shan Hutong, Chuan Dian Hutong, Ri Sheng Hutong, Yue Guang Hutong); personage and family name (Zhang Zizhong Lu, Jia Jia Hutong); market and merchandise (Cai Shi Kou Hutong, Yin Wan Hutong); factory and workshop (Da Mo Chang, You Qi Zuo Hutong); flower, grass, fish and insect (Hua Zhi Hutong, Cao Yuan Hutong, Jin Yu Hutong, Yang Feng Jiadao); cloud, rain, star, and sky (Yun Ju Hutong, Yu Er Hutong, Da Xing Hutong, Kong Chang); chicken, duck, fish, and meat (Ji Zhua Hutong, Ya Zi Dian, Xian Yu Kou, Rou Shi Jie) and so forth. Though being diversified, the dazzling multitude of names are subject to their own inherent laws when they are carefully analyzed.

Names of Hutongs in Beijing were actually centering around men. Some Hutongs were directly called by the names of noted personages. Many others, though not being called by names of persons, were the locations of former residences of notables, such as the former residence of Kang Youwei is in Mi Shi Hutong; the former residence of Tan Sitong in Bei Ban Jie Hutong; the Guild of

Zhongshan County in Zhu Chao Jie, where Dr. Sun Yat-sen had visited; the house in Xiao Yang Jia Hutong, where Mr. Lao She was born; the former residence of Mei Lanfang in Hu Guo Si Jie; the former residence of Mao Dun in Hou Yuan En Si Hutong; the former residence of Cheng Yanqiu in Lane No.3 to the north of Xisi; and so on. A large part of names were directly related to daily lives of people on the spheres of basic necessities of life. The names of Hutongs in Beijing fall roughly into 4 categories; 1. Those named by the names of persons; 2. Those named by merchandise; 3. Those named by buildings; and 4. Those named by terrains and scenes.

Nearly 150 pictures are collected in this album, depicting from different angles the features of Hutongs belonging separately to these 4 categories. They cover only a very small proportion of the actually existing ones because the spaces are limited. We just want to provide readers with a summary concept about Hutongs of Beijing.

一、胡同之最

The "Mosts" of Hutongs in Beijing

老北京人说："北京的胡同有名的三百六，无名的似牛毛。"意思是说北京的胡同多得数不清。虽不免有些夸张，却也反映出北京胡同的浩繁散乱，多姿多彩。看了北京现存最古老的、最长的、最短的、最宽的、最窄的、拐弯最多的胡同，看到至今仍保留下的有过街楼的胡同、有木牌楼的胡同、有琉璃牌楼的胡同、有拱门砖雕的胡同等，您除了能感受到老北京的居住生活特色与情趣，还会不会引发出更深刻的思索呢？

A saying goes among old Beijing residents that, in Beijing, 360 Hutongs are given a name each, while those without names are beyond calculation "Like ox hair", meaning that Hutongs in Beijing are innumerable. Though being exaggerated, Hutongs in Beijing are really numerous and present different features. Look at the examples; The existing most ancient ones, the longest ones, the shortest ones, the broadest ones, the most narrow ones, those with largest number of turns, as well as those existing ones with spanning overhead building projections, those with wooden monuments, those with glazed monuments, those with houses decorated by arched gateways and carved bricks, and so forth. Do they arouse deeper thinking in addition to learning about the features and interests of the lives of old residents in Beijing?

北京现今最长的胡同之一：东西交民巷，全长3公里

Being 3 km in length, Dong/Xi Jiao Min Xiang is one of the longest Hutongs in Beijing now.

北京最短的胡同之一：一尺大街仅长25.23米 (现已并到杨梅竹斜街)

Being only 25.23 m in length, thus one of the shortest Hutongs in Beijing in former days, Yi Chi Da Jie has been combined with Yang Mei Zhu Xiejie.

北京现存最古老的胡同之一：元朝就有的砖塔胡同

Zhuan Ta Hutong, formed in Yuan Dynasty, is one of the oldest Hutongs in Beijing.

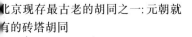

1

3

2

1. 北京现今最窄的胡同之一:小喇叭胡同(北口尚不足0.6米)

Being less than 0.6m at its northern end, Xiao La Ba Hutong is one of the most narrow Hutongs in present-day Beijing.

2. 北京现今最宽的胡同之一:灵境胡同(最宽处达32.18米)

Ling Jing Hutong, being 32.18 m at its widest part, is one of the broadest Hutongs in Beijing now.

3. 北京胡同中仅存的过街楼:儒福里的观音院过街楼

The Only Existing Spanning Overhead Building Projection in Guan Yin Yuan, Ru Fu Li, Beijing

4. 北京胡同中仅存的琉璃牌坊:神路街北的东岳庙牌坊

Dong Yue Miao Pailou at the north side of Shen Lu Jie is the only existing glazed Pailou in a Hutong of Beijing.

5. 北京现今拐弯最多的胡同之一:九湾胡同

Jiu Wan Hutong, A Lane with the Largest Number of Turns in Beijing now

4

5

北京胡同中尚存的拱门砖雕: 东棉花
胡同15号院内的拱门砖雕
The arched gate with carved bricks in
No.15, Dong Mian Hua Hutong, is the
only existing one in a Hutong of
Beijing

北京胡同中现存的木牌楼: 国子监街
东口成贤街牌楼
The only existing wooden Pailou in
Beijing is Located at Cheng Xian Jie
Eastern End of Guo Zi Jian Jie.

二、以人名命名
的胡同

Hutongs Called by Names
of Persons

在前言中已经提到过，北京的胡同名称实际上是以人为中心的，直接以人名、姓氏命名的胡同就有百十来条。既有以人们所敬仰的民族英雄的名字来命名的，也有几个朝代的历史名人、达官贵人的名字来命名的，然而数量最多的还是以平民百姓、小商小贩、小手工业者的姓名来命名的，因为他们的所做所为，与胡同里居住的普通老百姓的生活更为接近。这类胡同名称充分体现出人文倾向。

As mentioned in the foreword, names of Hutongs in Beijing were actually centering around men. Over 100 Hutongs are called directly by names or house names. These include names of national heroes who have been admired and respected by the people, names of historic notables and VIPs of several dynasties, while most are names of common people, pedlars and craftsmen because they are most closely related to inhabitants in the lanes. Such names of Hutongs fully present a humane inclination.

文丞相胡同:以南宋抗元丞相文天祥
的官称命名的胡同
Wen Cheng Xiang Hutong, Named by
the Official Position of Wen Tianxiang,
the Southern Song Prime Minister
Who Fought against the Yuan Invaders

中毛家湾
Zhong Mao Jia Wan

潘家胡同(原称潘家河沿)
Pan Jia Hutong
(Originally Called Pan Jia He Yan)

红星胡同(原称吴良大人胡同)
Hong Xing Hutong (originally Called
Wu Liang Da Ren Hutong)

1.赵登禹路:以抗日爱国将领赵登禹将军的名字命名的胡同

Zhao Dengyu Lu was named after the name of a patriotic general who fought bravely against Japanese invaders in the War of Resistance.

2.遂安伯胡同:以明朝功臣陈志的封爵命名的胡同

Sui An Bo Hutong was named after the title of Chen Zhi, a high official who made meritorious contributions in Ming Dynasty.

3.刘海胡同(原称刘汉胡同)

Liu Hai Hutong(Originally Called Liu Han Hutong)

4.大木仓北二巷:原称郑王府夹道,是以清朝八家"铁帽王"之一和硕郑亲王济尔哈朗的王府命名的胡同

Da Mu Cang Bei Er Xiang was originally called Zheng Wang Fu Jiadao. Zheng Wang Fu referred to the residence of Jierhalang (Heshuo Prince Zheng) who was one of the 8 Tiemaowang's (Eternal Princedom) in Qing Dynasty.

5.刘兰塑胡同:以元朝著名塑像家刘元的名字命名的胡同,曾讹传为刘銮塑或琉璃塑

Liu Lan Su Hutong is called by the name of Liu Yuan, a famous statue engraver of Yuan Dynasty, The name had been passed erroneously as Liu Luan Su or Liu Li Su.

6.张自忠路:以抗日名将张自忠的名字命名的胡同

Zhang Zizhong Lu was named after the famous general who fought against Japanese invaders.

7.韩家胡同(原称韩家潭)

Han Jia Hutong(Originally Called Han Jia Tan)

8.三不老胡同:以明朝三保太监郑和的官称三保太监命名的胡同,后讹为三保老爹胡同

San Bu Lao Hutong was named after the official title of Zheng He (San Bao Eunuch of Ming Dynasty), and spread erroneously as San Bao Lao Die Hutong.

1

2

史家胡同
Shi Jia Hutong

外交部街：原名石大人胡同，是以明朝
大将石亨的官称命名的胡同

Wai Jiao Bu Jie was originally named
Shi Da Ren Hutong after the title of
Shi Heng, a general of Ming Dynasty.

育芳胡同(原称班大人胡同)
Yu Fang Hutong (originally
Called Ban Da Ren Hutong)

武定胡同：以明初开国功臣郭英的后代世袭封爵武定侯命名的胡同，原称武定侯胡同

Wu Ding Hutong was originally called Wu Ding Hou Hutong which was named after the granted title of Marquis Wu Ding inherited by the offsprings of Guo Ying, a high official who made meritorious contributions for the founding of Ming Dynasty.

三、以市场商品命名的胡同

Hutongs Called by Names of Markets and Merchandise

在胡同中居住的老百姓日常生活是离不开必需的商品的，因而就有了不少以商品来命名的胡同。而买卖商品自然又离不开市场，所以又有了以市场来命名的胡同。尽管随着时代的变迁，有些早年间的市场和商品早已失去了它原本的意义，或不复存在了。可其旧名称依然如故地沿用了下来，而且这样的胡同名称至今仍存在着不少，它们反映出北京居民时代生活的横断面。

People living in Hutongs need necessary merchandise in their daily lives and trading needs markets, hence the names of such Hutongs. Many such names have been kept though markets and merchandise of old times had long lost their original significances. They present the sectional phases of epochal lives of Beijing inhabitants.

钱市胡同
Qian Shi Hutong

胭脂胡同中一个院门的门铍
The Knockers on the Door of A Courtyard in Yan Zhi Hutong

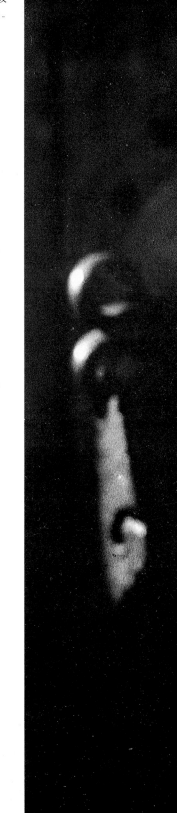

育强胡同(原称椒园厂、猪毛厂)
Yu Qiang Hutong
(Originally Called Jiao Yuan Chang, or
Zhu Mao Chang)

1 廊房二条
Lang Fang Er Tiao

2 廊房头条
Lang Fang Tou Tiao

3 西四北三条(原称箔子胡同)
Xi Si Bei San Tiao
(Originally Called Bo Zi Hutong)

1

2

3

宗帽四条

Zong Mao Si Tiao

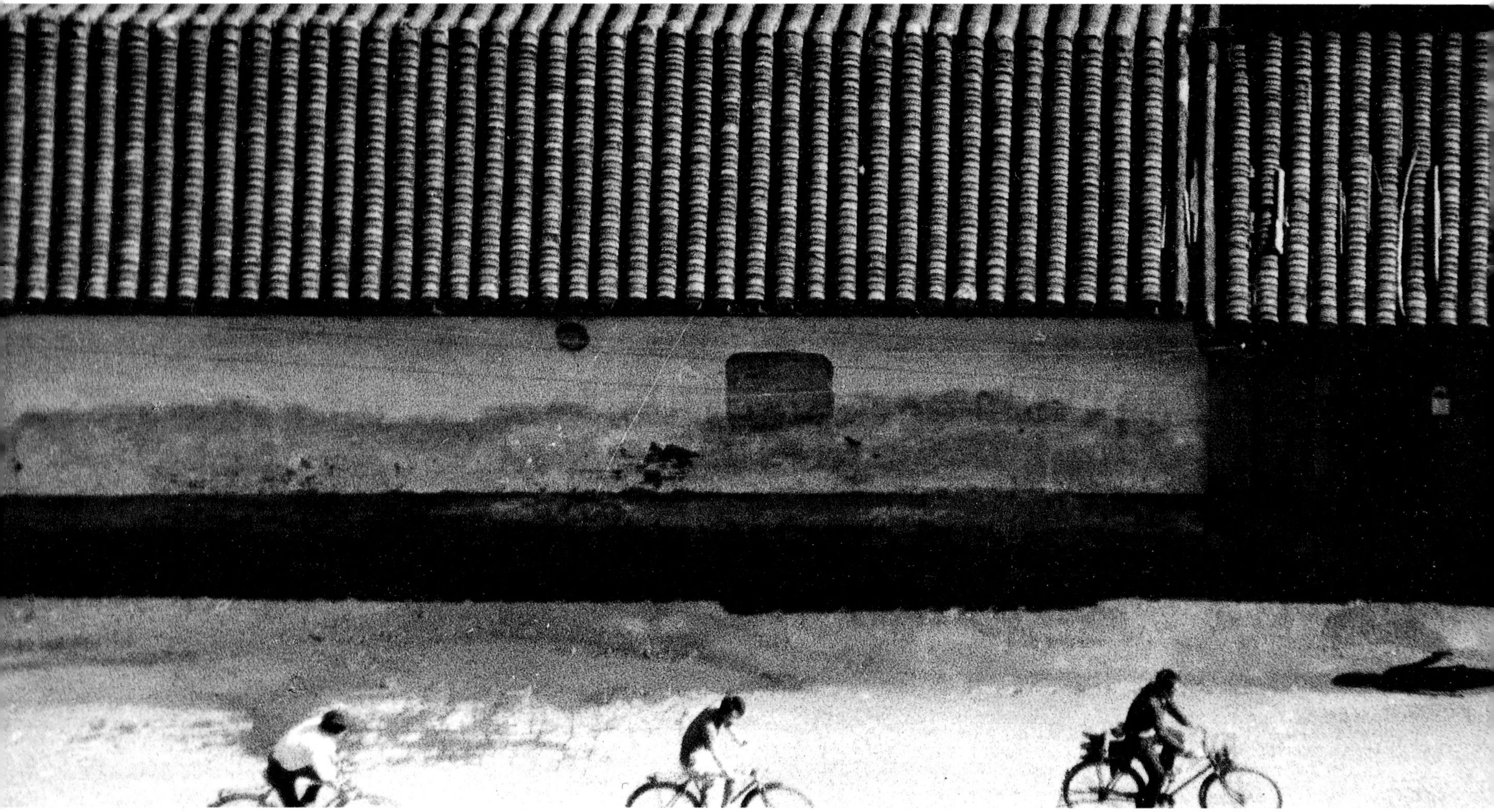

珠市口东大街中的小巷
A Small Lane in Zhu Shi Kou Dong
Dajie

辟才胡同(原称劈柴胡同)
Pi Cai Hutong
(Originally Called Pi Chai Hutong)

小绒线胡同

Xiao Rong Xian Hutong

煤渣胡同
Mei Zha Hutong

毡子胡同
Zhan Zi Hutong

花市上三条一户人家的烟筒
Stovepipe of A Household in Hua Shi
Shang Santiao

琉璃厂东街
Liu Li Chang Dong Jie

牛街
Niu Jie

48

官菜园上街
Guang Cai Yuan Shang Jie

菜市口胡同
Cai Shi Kou Hutong

49

大茶叶胡同
Da Cha Ye Hutong

灯市口北巷
Deng Shi Kou Bei Xiang

花市中二条墙上的儿童画

Children's Picture on the Wall, Hua
Shi Zhong Ertiao

草厂北巷
Cao Chang Bei Xiang

四、以建筑物命名
的胡同

Hutongs with Names
Taken from Buildings

北京各式各样的建筑物，也与胡同里的老百姓日常生活密切相关。而且这些建筑物又都非常显见，离着大老远的就能看得到，便于寻找，所以许多胡同就以这些建筑物来命名了。建筑物所包涵的面非常广泛，不仅包括高大的城门、古老的寺庙、漂亮的花园、幽深的府邸、各地的会馆，也含有各种官家机构、工厂、作坊、仓库、还有一些特殊场所等等。这些建筑绝不仅仅只是宏伟庄严或美丽幽静的物，它们之所以能成为流传儿百年的胡同名称，更重要的则是历史文化。

Various kinds of buildings in Beijing are also closely related to daily lives of common people. Generally, such buildings are so conspicuously located that they could be seen from afar, and are easy to find. "Building" includes a wide range of contents—towering city gates, ancient temples, beautiful gardens, secluded residences, guilds of different places, as well as official organizations, factories, workshops, warehouses and some special arenas. These buildings are not only taken as magnificent or beautiful objects. What is more important in making them names of Hutongs that prevailed for several hundred years is historic culture.

内务部街(原称勾栏胡同)中的一个门楼
An Arched Gateway in Nei Wu Bu Jie Which Was Originally called Gou Lan Hutong

小院胡同中一个院门的门槛和台阶
Steps and Wooden Threshold in Front of the Gateway of A Courtyard in Xiao Yuan Hutong

宫门口三条俯瞰
Panoramic View of Gong Men Kou Santiao

东廊下胡同
Dong Lang Xia Hutong

云居胡同(原称云居寺胡同)
Yun Ju Hutong
(Originally Called Yun Ju Si Hutong)

5

6

1.白塔寺东夹道
Bai Ta Si Dong Jia Dao

2.护国寺西巷中的屋脊、房檐
Ridges and Eaves of a House in Hu Guo Si Xi Xiang

3.法源寺前街
Fa Yuan Si Qian Jie

4.护国寺西巷
Hu Guo Si Xi Xiang

5.护国寺街中的摊车
Pedlars' Cart in Hu Guo Si Jie

6.新太仓胡同雨景
Xin Tai Cang Hutong in Rain

7.老墙根街中的摊位
Pedlars in Lao Qiang Gen Jie

8.隆福寺街
Long Fu Si Jie

9.演乐胡同
Yan Yue Hutong

7

8

9

朝阳门北小街
Chao Yang Men Bei Xiao Jie

白塔寺西夹道
Bai Ta Si Xi Jia Dao

1. 东不压桥胡同(原称东步粮桥胡同)
Dong Bu Ya Qiao Hutong
(Originally Called Dong Bu Liang
Qiao Hutong)

2. 会计司胡同中的一个院门
The Gate of A Courtyard in Kuai Ji Si
Hutong

3. 府学胡同
Fu Xue Hutong

4. 宫门口东岔的瓜摊(宫门口是以朝
天宫命名的)
Melon Seller in the Eastern Branch
Lane of Gong Men Kou ("Gong"
refers to Chao Tian Gong)

校尉营胡同中的老人与鸟笼
Old Man and Bird-Cages in Xiao Wei
Ying Hutong

锻库胡同
Duan Ku Hutong

铸钟胡同
Zhu Zhong Hutong

旧鼓楼大街
Jiu Gu Lou Da Jie

澡堂子胡同(现已并入到珠市口东大
街)
Zao Tang Zi Hutong
(Now Being Combined with Zhu Shi
Kou Dong Dajie)

五、以地形景物等命名的胡同

Hutongs Named by Terrains and Scenes

北京的地势大体上是西北高,东南低,而原来的外城,在元、明时尚是一片水乡洼地。城里也有不少明河暗沟流过,后被填平成了胡同,其名称就以原水道来命名了。在这些河道走向影响下,也使原本状如棋盘的总体胡同格局中,出现了一些斜街,为了给人以明示就直称为斜街。还有更直接地以这条胡同本身的形状命名的,或以胡同中存在的桥、井、树等标志命名的。因其依据是众所瞩目,且长久不易改变的客观实体,所以这类用直呼其名的方式命名的胡同,都叫得较为长久和稳定,关键在于大家都乐意接受。

The terrain of Beijing inclines from the northwest down to the southeast. In Yuan and Ming Dynasties when the site later became the outer city was yet a vast span of watery low-lying land, many surface rivers and underground streams flowed through the inner city. Those rivers and streams were filled up and made into Hutongs, and the original names of watercourses were taken as names of related Hutongs. Under such circumstances, some slanting streets appeared among the original chessboard setup, Such streets were named Xie Jie to provide passers-by with distinct directions. Some names directly indicated the forms of the Hutongs, and others were named after the bridges, wells or trees existing in the Hutongs. Such names have been well-received because they came from objective substances which attracted people's attentions and were not so easy to change within a considerable length of time, thus they can exist steadily and much longer.

高井胡同
Gao Jing Hutong

70

青竹巷
Qing Zhu Xiang

水车胡同
Shui Che Hutong

后抄手胡同
Hou Chao Shou Hutong

后海夹道
Hou Hai Jia Dao

4

5

1.万源夹道
Wan Yuan Jia Dao

2.朱苇箔胡同(原称猪尾巴胡同)
Zhu Wei Bo Hutong
(Originally Called Zhu Wei Ba Hutong)

3.千竿胡同
Qian Gan Hutong

4.贯通巷
Guan Tong Xiang

5.门框胡同
Men Kuang Hutong

6.留题胡同(原称牛蹄胡同)
Liu Ti Hutong.
(Originally Called Niu Ti Hutong)

6

树荫胡同
Shu Yin Hutong

后车胡同
Hou Che Hutong

铁影壁胡同旧照
An Old Photograph of the Lane

铁影壁胡同
Tie Ying Bi Hutong

什锦花园胡同
Shi Jin Hua Yuan Hutong

1.崇文门西河沿
Chong Wen Men Xi He Yan

2.东轿杆胡同
Dong Jiao Gan Hutong

1

2

3

3.核桃巷
He Tao Xiang

4.八宝坑胡同
Ba Bao Keng Hutong

4

81

前车胡同
Qian Che Hutong

西斜往
Xi Xiej

大石桥胡同
Da Shi Qiao Hutong

九道湾北巷
Jiu Dao Wan Bei Xiang

四川营
Si Chuan Ying

大栅栏
Da Zha Lan

大沟巷
Da Gou Xiang

小椅子圈胡同
Xiao Yi Zi Quan Hutong

小杨家胡同(原称小羊圈胡同)是著名
作家老舍先生的出生地
Xiao Yang Jia Hutong
(Originally Called Xiao Yang Quan
Hutong)
It was the site where locates the
house in which Mr. Lao She, the
famous writer, was born.

铃铛胡同
Ling Dang Hutong

板桥头条
Ban Qiao Tou Tiao

大菊胡同
Da Ju Hutong

井楼胡同
Jing Lou Hutong

北京的胡同　Hutongs of Beijing